LOOK IT UP
Now in a fully revised edition

1. You and Your Body
2. People and Customs
3. What People Do
4. The Prehistoric World
5. Ships and Boats
6. People of Long Ago
7. The Sea
8. The Earth
9. Cold-Blooded Animals
10. Warm-Blooded Animals
11. Sport and Entertainment
12. The World of Machines
13. Land Travel
14. Flying
15. Outer Space
16. Index

Photo Credits: Heather Angel, M.Sc.,F.R.P.S.; Australian News and Information Bureau; British Tourist Authority; Camerapix Hutchison Library; Central Office of Information; Douglas Dickins F.R.P.S.; Robert Estall; Michael Holford; Eric and David Hosking; Koninklijke Adriaan Volker Groep; Tony Loftas; Denis Marshall; Cees van der Meulen; Natural History Photographic Agency; Picturepoint; BBC Hulton Pictury Library; G.R.Roberts; Seaphot; The Viking Ship Museum, Denmark; ZEFA.

Front cover: Bruce Colman.

Illustrators: Fred Anderson; Linda Broad; Mike Chappell; Richard Eastland; Elizabeth Graham-Yool; Colin Hawkins; Illustra; Ron Haywood; Eric Jewell; Vanessa Luff; Ben Manchipp; Stephanie Manchipp; David Palmer; Mike Roffe; Laura Rogers; Esther Rowley; Temple Art; George Thompson; Raymond Turvey.

First edition © Macmillan Publishers Limited, 1979
Reprinted in 1981, 1982, 1983 and 1984
Second edition © Macmillan Publishers Limited, 1985

All rights reserved. No reproduction, copy or transmission of this publication in any form or by any means, may be made without written permission

Chief Educational Adviser
Lynda Snowdon

Teacher Advisory Panel
Helen Craddock, John Enticknap, Arthur Razzell

Editorial Board
Jan Burgess, Rosemary Canter, Philip M. Clark, Beatrice Phillpotts, Sue Seddon, Philip Steele

Picture Researchers
Caroline Adams, Anne Marie Ehrlich, Gayle Hayter, Ethel Hurwicz, Pat Hodgson, Stella Martin, Frances Middlestorb

Designer
Keith Faulkner

Contributors and consultants
John E. Allen, Neil Ardley, Sue Becklake, Robert Burton, Barry Cox, Jacqueline Dineen, David J. Fletcher, Plantagenet Somerset Fry, Bill Gunston, Robin Kerrod, Mark Lambert, Anne Millard, Kaye Orten, Ian Ridpath, Peter Stephens, Nigel Swann, Aubrey Tulley, Tom Williamson, Thomas Wright

Published by Macmillan Children's Books
a division of Macmillan Publishers Limited
4 Little Essex Street, London WC2R 3LF
Associated companies throughout the world

ISBN 0 333 39725 8 (volume 7)
ISBN 0 333 39568 9 (complete set)

Printed in Hong Kong

The Sea

Second Edition
LOOK IT UP

Contents

	Page
WHAT IS THE SEA?	4
A day at the seaside	4
How the oceans began	6
Underneath the sea	8
The salty sea	10
WHAT LIVES IN THE SEA?	12
Animals of the seashore	12
Rocky shores	14
Estuaries	16
Coral reefs	18
Icy seas	20
Deep oceans	22
THE POWER OF THE SEA	24
The Beaufort scale	26
Tides	28
Currents	30
How the sea wears away the land	32

	Page
SAFETY AT SEA	**34**
Sea rescue	36
Ports and harbours	38
RICHES FROM THE SEA	**40**
Deep-sea fishing	42
Fish farming	44
Treasures from the sea	46
PEOPLE AND THE SEA	**48**
Homes under the sea	50
Save our seas	52
Taking land from the sea	54
THE SEA IN HISTORY	**56**
Myths and stories about the sea	56
Sea battles	58
The navigators	60
Pirates	62
DID YOU KNOW?	**64**
INDEX	

WHAT IS THE SEA?

A day at the seaside

Many people enjoy holidays by the sea. It is fun to go swimming and play games on the sand. Most people who swim in the sea stay near the shore. Further out to sea, people sail dinghies and other small boats. Lighthouses warn bigger ships to keep away from rocks.

It is enjoyable to go swimming in the sea but the sea has other uses too. Many kinds of animals live in the sea. People catch fish for food. Big ships carry cargo and passengers around the world. Oil is drilled from the sea bed.

How the oceans began

Long before there were any animals or people in the world, the earth was made of very hot rocks. As the rocks cooled down, they gave off steam. The steam turned into water which collected in deep holes on the earth's surface. This water formed the seas and oceans. The high parts of the earth were left as dry land.

When water is boiled in a kettle, it makes a cloud of steam. If the steam touches a cold window pane or mirror, it turns to water. The water runs down the mirror in tiny drops, just like rain.

Land and sea are not spread evenly over the earth. Here you can see more land than sea. The large areas of land are called continents.

The sun heats the water in the sea. The water turns into vapour, which gathers in clouds. When the clouds rise they meet cold air. Cold air turns the vapour back into water and so rain falls in the sea.

In other parts of the world there is not much land. The large seas are called oceans. There are four oceans in the world.

If all the land were joined together we would see that most of the earth is covered by water. The earth is sometimes called the Blue Planet, because of all the water.

Underneath the sea

Most people at the seaside see only the surface of the sea. People who dive underwater find many different creatures and other exciting things. There are fish of all kinds. Some are very colourful. There are dolphins and turtles and other strange creatures. Some divers search for pearls in oysters.

The bottom of the sea is called the sea bed. When the tide goes out, part of the sea bed is uncovered. If the tide went out far enough, this island would become a hill. It is really part of the land.

The salty sea

If you dip your finger in the sea and then lick it, it will taste salty. Water in rivers, ponds and lakes is not salty. It is fresh. The salt in sea water comes from the rocks in the earth's surface and from volcanoes. The salt is very important to animals living in the sea. These animals would die without salt.

Shipwrecked sailors get very thirsty. They cannot drink sea water because the salt would make them ill.

Some seabirds can drink sea water. They have a special way of getting the salt out of their bodies.

The salt in the sea is the same salt that we put on our food. In some places salt is made by collecting sea water in shallow pools called saltpans. The hot sun dries up the pools and salt is left behind.

In the picture below, people are working in saltpans in Morocco.

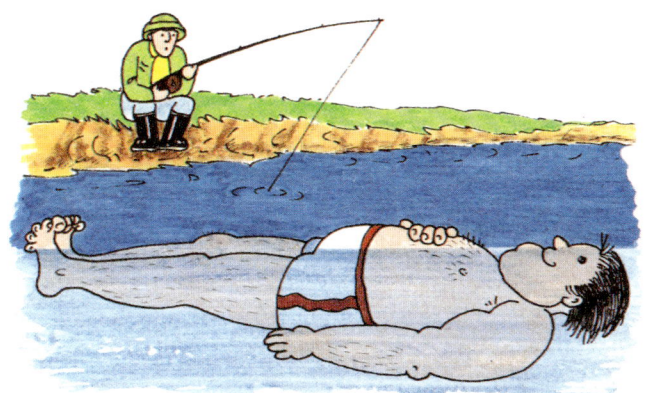

Fresh water has no salt in it. It is lighter than sea water. It is difficult to float in fresh water.

The salt in sea water makes the water heavier than fresh water. You can float easily in sea water.

The water in the Dead Sea is very salty indeed. People can sit up and read the newspaper while they float.

WHAT LIVES IN THE SEA?

Animals of the seashore

The sea is full of different kinds of animals. Many of them live near the shore. Seashores covered with sand or pebbles are called beaches. Other seashores are covered with rocks or mud. Each kind of seashore has its own animals living on it.

Very few animals can live on pebbly beaches like this one. When the tide is in, the waves roll the pebbles around. This makes it difficult for animals to find places to hide for protection. Only a few tiny creatures can hide safely under the pebbles. It is hard to find them.

oyster-catcher

tube-worm

shrimp

cockle

In the big picture you can see some of the animals which live on the seashore. Cockles and razor-shells live under the sand. Starfish, prawns and small fish are brought in by the tide. Sea anemones live on the rocks. Oyster-catchers look for food at low tide. They eat shellfish.

A sandy beach is a good place for animals to live. At low tide you cannot see them because they hide under the sand. If you dig a deep hole you will find some animals. There will be worms, crabs and shellfish. When the tide comes in these animals come out to feed.

Rocky shores

The best place to look for animals is on a rocky shore. Some animals cling on to the rocks or hide under seaweed. Other animals live in pools of water, left behind when the tide goes out. If you look carefully you can find many different kinds of animals in rock pools.

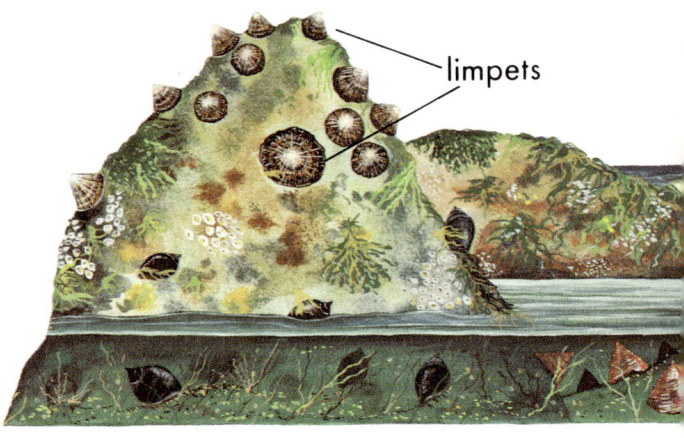

The creatures and plants in the picture above are uncovered by the tide each day.

Small fish, like the rock goby and the sea scorpion, are trapped in rock pools at low tide.

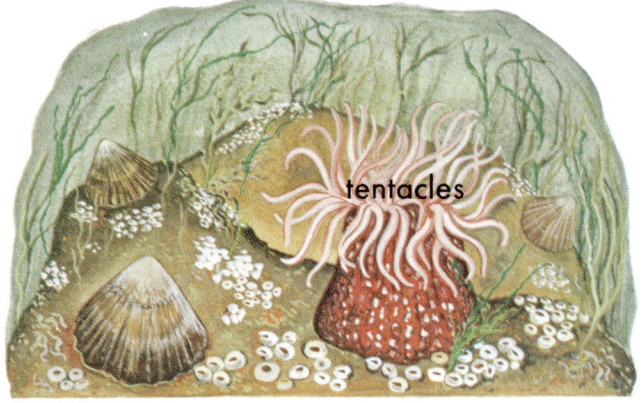

Sea anemones look like plants but they are animals. They use their tentacles to catch food.

When the tide is out, seaweed hangs down and limpets cling to the rocks. Only a hard knock will get them off.

Rock gobies use their fins to cling tightly to the rocks. They cannot be swept away when the waves rush over the shore. Starfish cling to rocks as well.

On rocky coasts like this one there are often steep cliffs and small bays called coves. Most sea animals live in coves. The coves shelter them from the biggest waves.

Estuaries

An estuary is the place where a river meets the sea. Salty sea water mixes with fresh water from the river. This mixed water is less salty than sea water.

The river leaves mud and sand along the banks of the estuary. Many animals live in these mud and sand banks. Estuaries are important because they make good sheltered harbours.

When the tide is in, sea water fills up the estuary and flows into the river.

At low tide, mud and sand are uncovered. Fresh water from the river flows out to sea. Animals come to feed on the mud and sand banks.

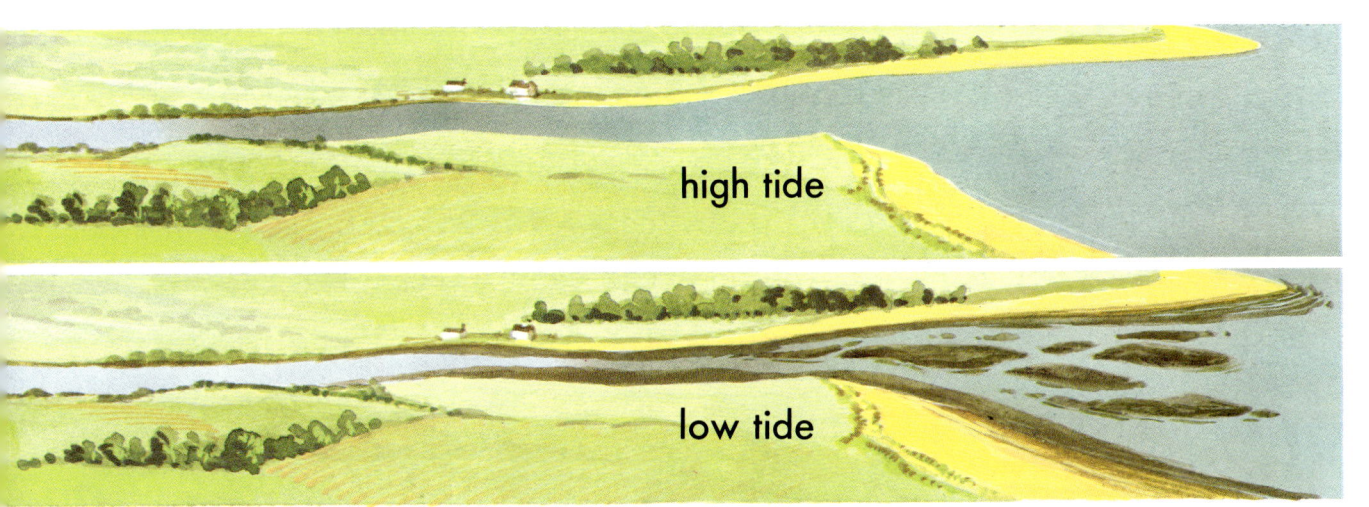

Animals which live in estuaries are in fresh water at low tide. When the tide comes in the water gets more salty. These animals are able to live in both kinds of water.

17

Coral reefs

The warm seas around Australia are famous for their coral reefs. Coral is made from the skeletons of tiny animals, which can only live in very warm seas. Many colourful animals live in reefs.

Sea slugs are like the slugs you sometimes see in the countryside. Sea slugs eat seaweed, sea anemones and jellyfish.

The beautiful spotted lionfish in the picture below is dangerous. It has poisonous spines on its back.

This coral island is part of the Great Barrier Reef of Australia.

The hawkfish perches on a lump of coral, waiting for food to float past.

The long-nosed butterfly fish pokes into deep cracks in the coral reef, looking for small animals to eat.

Coral animals are like tiny sea anemones but they have skeletons. When they die, their skeletons are left behind and form reefs.

long-nosed butterfly fish

Icy seas

The Arctic and the Antarctic are very cold parts of the world. The sea freezes over, forming great sheets of ice. Some animals can live in the cold. Eskimo people live in some parts of the Arctic and hunt the animals.

Icebergs are huge lumps of ice which break off glaciers and float out to sea. Glaciers are frozen masses of snow. Some icebergs are many kilometres wide.

seals

Only a small part of an iceberg is above water. Most of it is hidden below the water line. This hidden ice can be very dangerous to ships. Sometimes pieces of ice, called icefloes, break off from the frozen sea.

Seals, polar bears and seabirds live in the Arctic. Thick layers of fat in their bodies keep them warm. The polar bears eat seals.

black guillemots

polar bear

We do not know much about the great continent of Antarctica at the South Pole. Countries send men to carry out scientific experiments to find out more. The men travel in special ships like this one.

Deep oceans
In the middle of the oceans the water is very deep. Different kinds of fish live at different depths. On the surface there are flying fish and insects such as ocean striders. Near the bottom there are some very strange looking fish. It is so dark that many of them are completely blind.

22

THE POWER OF THE SEA

The sea can be very dangerous during storms. Strong winds make high waves which are very powerful. These waves can damage ships. They fill the ships with water until they sink. Storms can cause flooding too. Houses near the coast are sometimes completely wrecked during floods.

It is very dangerous if a ship's engines stop in a storm. Waves batter the ship and water pours over the deck. If the ship's pumps are not working, the ship will sink. The old painting below shows a paddle steamer in a storm. Another boat has come to its rescue.

Flat lands are always in danger of being swamped by swollen rivers and rough seas. When a storm and a very high tide happen together, they can cause very bad flooding. Sometimes buildings and crops are destroyed and people are made homeless. Boats have to be used to rescue people and animals from the floods. The floods on the left are in Thailand.

Storms are particularly dangerous when ships are near rocks. This ship is stuck on rocks near the coast. When ships are wrecked near the shore, the crew can usually be saved. Lifeboats go out to rescue the men on board.

The Beaufort scale

Waves are made by the wind blowing the surface of the sea. Sailors need to know how strong the wind is. The force of the wind is measured by the Beaufort scale.

At Force 0 there is no wind at all. The sea is completely calm.

At Force 1 you can just see tiny waves on the sea.

At Force 2 there is only a very gentle wind blowing.

At Force 3 small flags flap in the wind.

At Force 4 leaves are blown around. Small branches move in the wind.

At Force 5 small trees sway and large waves break on the shore.

At Force 6 a strong wind is blowing. You can see large flags flapping.

As the wind blows harder, the waves get bigger. When the wind has died down, the waves go on spreading across the sea. These waves are called swell.

At Force 7 a gale is blowing. Foam is blown from the waves.

At Force 8 the gale is getting strong. Twigs break off trees.

At Force 9 the gale is strong. The wind blows slates from roofs.

At Force 10 the gale uproots trees and many houses are damaged. It is very difficult to see things clearly.

At Force 11 the storm is so strong that everything is in danger. Houses and trees are destroyed.

At Force 12 there is a hurricane. There are huge waves, and houses and trees are washed away.

Tides

Tides are caused by the sun and the moon attracting the sea towards them. The tide comes in and goes out twice a day. At high tide, the sea is much further up the beach than at low tide.

Sometimes there is a great difference between high and low tide. This is the Bay of Fundy at low tide.

This is the Bay of Fundy at high tide. The water is 12 metres higher than at low tide.

When the sun and moon are in line, they attract the sea together, and make the tide full. These large tides are called Spring tides.

During the year the sun and moon sometimes attract the sea in different directions. Then there is only a small difference between high and low tides. These are the Neap Tides.

Mont St Michel is an island in France. When the tide is low, you can walk to it across the sand. At high tide the island is completely surrounded by water.

Currents

Currents are movements of water in the sea. They are sometimes more dangerous than winds and waves because you cannot see them.

Currents are there even when there is no wind. They can sweep ships onto rocks and carry swimmers and small boats out to sea.

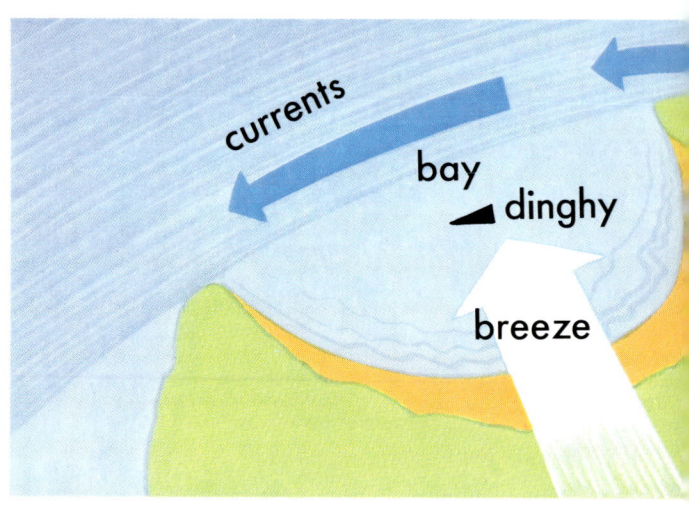

This boy has lost the oars of his rubber dinghy. His father is rushing to rescue him. Out of the bay, strong currents will carry him away. The sea can be dangerous – take care!

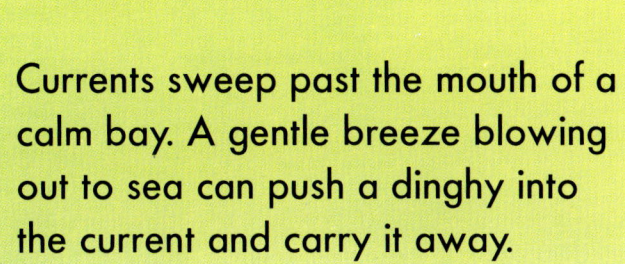

Currents sweep past the mouth of a calm bay. A gentle breeze blowing out to sea can push a dinghy into the current and carry it away.

A current goes faster when it has to squeeze through a narrow gap.

current

This current is flowing between an island and the mainland. It moves fast and is very dangerous. A very fast current is called a race.

Around the coast, most currents are caused by the tide. These currents sometimes change direction as the tide goes in and out.
Far out to sea there are bigger currents. They are caused by the wind always blowing in the same direction. Ships travel faster if they get in a current flowing the way they want to go.

31

How the sea wears away the land

Waves break constantly on the seashore and against the bottom of cliffs. Over the years the waves gradually wear the rocks down. Eventually even tall cliffs collapse into the sea. It takes much longer for the sea to wear away hard rocks than soft rocks.

Breakwaters and dykes are often built to protect land from the pounding waves.

The sea has scooped out soft rocks to make the bay at the top of this picture. The harder rocks are left behind and form cliffs.

1

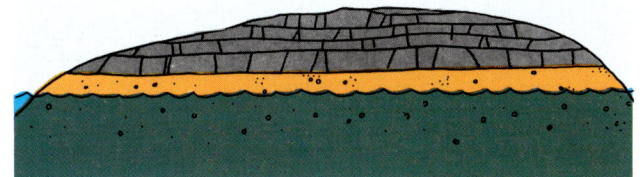

This island is made up of layers of different rocks.

2

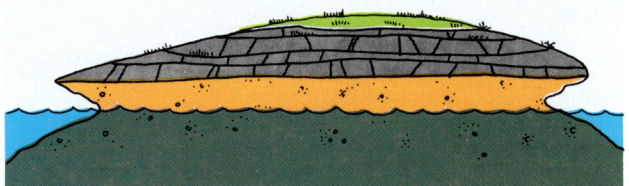

Gradually, the sea wears away the soft rocks around the island.

3

After a long time, a large amount of soft rock has been worn away.

4

This is Mushroom Island. Nearly all the soft rock has been worn away. One day this island will collapse into the sea.

SAFETY AT SEA

The sea can be very dangerous, so there are special services to help sailors. Buoys, lighthouses and lightships mark hidden rocks. Lifeboats, helicopters and special submarines help ships in trouble.

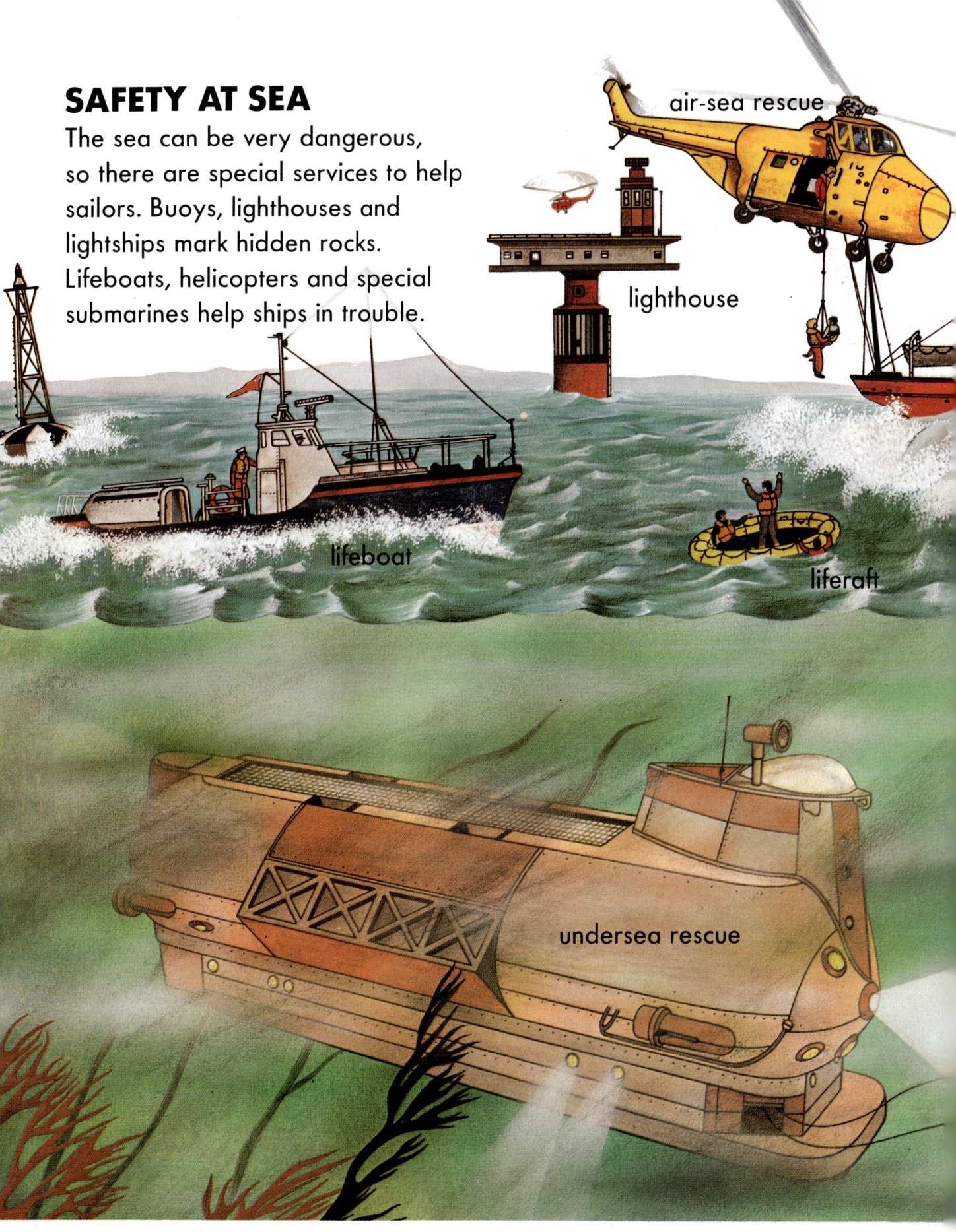

lightship

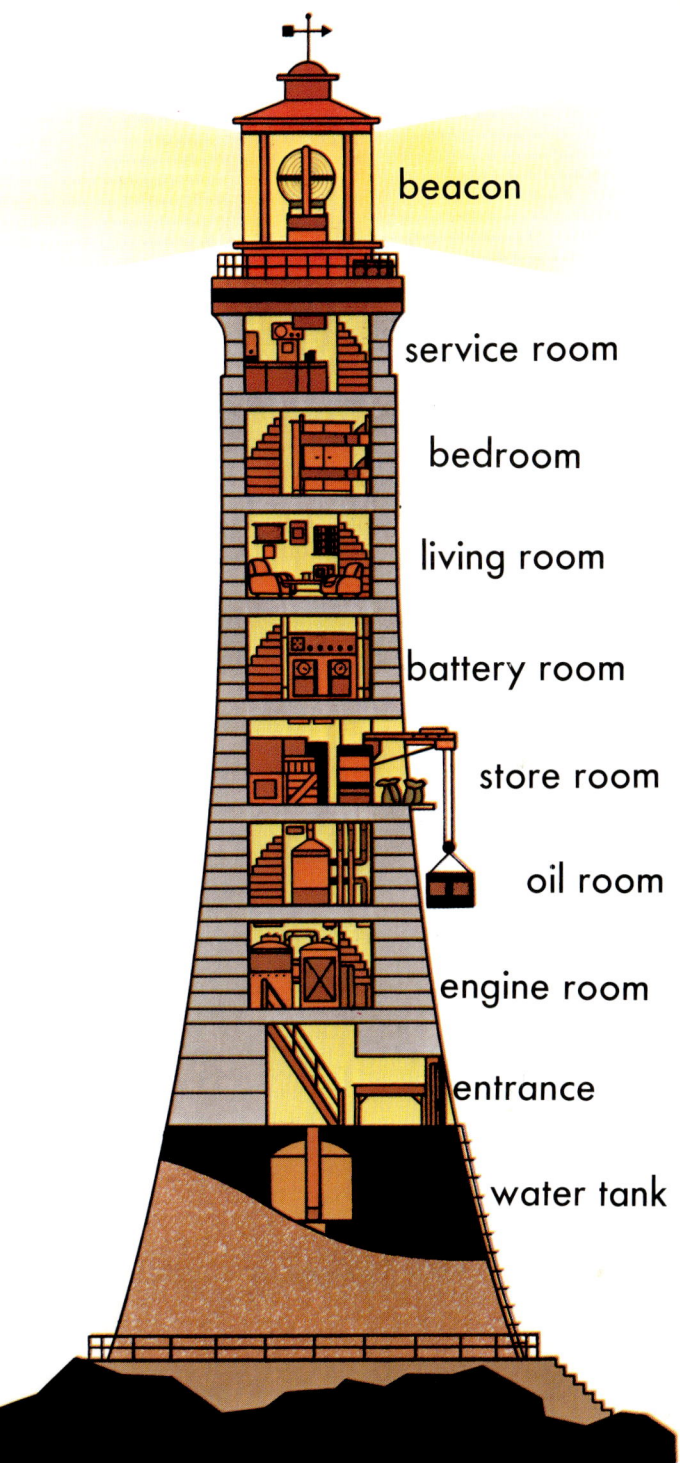

buoy

beacon
service room
bedroom
living room
battery room
store room
oil room
engine room
entrance
water tank

A lighthouse is a tall tower built on rocks or on a cliff. It warns ships to keep away. Powerful lights flash at night. Sometimes foghorns sound too. Bad weather often stops the lighthouse keeper from coming ashore. He has to store large supplies of food and water.

Sea rescue

When a ship sinks the sailors can sometimes save themselves. If there is time they can launch the ship's lifeboats or liferafts. The ship may sink so quickly that the men have to jump into the water. They wear lifejackets to keep them afloat. Other ships or special rescue services will pick them up.

Sometimes a ship sinks near a coast. A lifeboat comes out from the shore to rescue the sailors.

lifeboat

torch
batteries
hand flares
repair kit
parachute signals
first aid
seasick pills
life-line
liferaft
fishing line
hooks
oar
baler
water

Big ships carry liferafts. Food, water and equipment are kept on the liferaft. People can survive for many days until they are rescued.

The crew can be pulled to safety on a rope from a wreck on the shore.

This injured man is on a stretcher. A helicopter will haul him up from the ship and take him ashore.

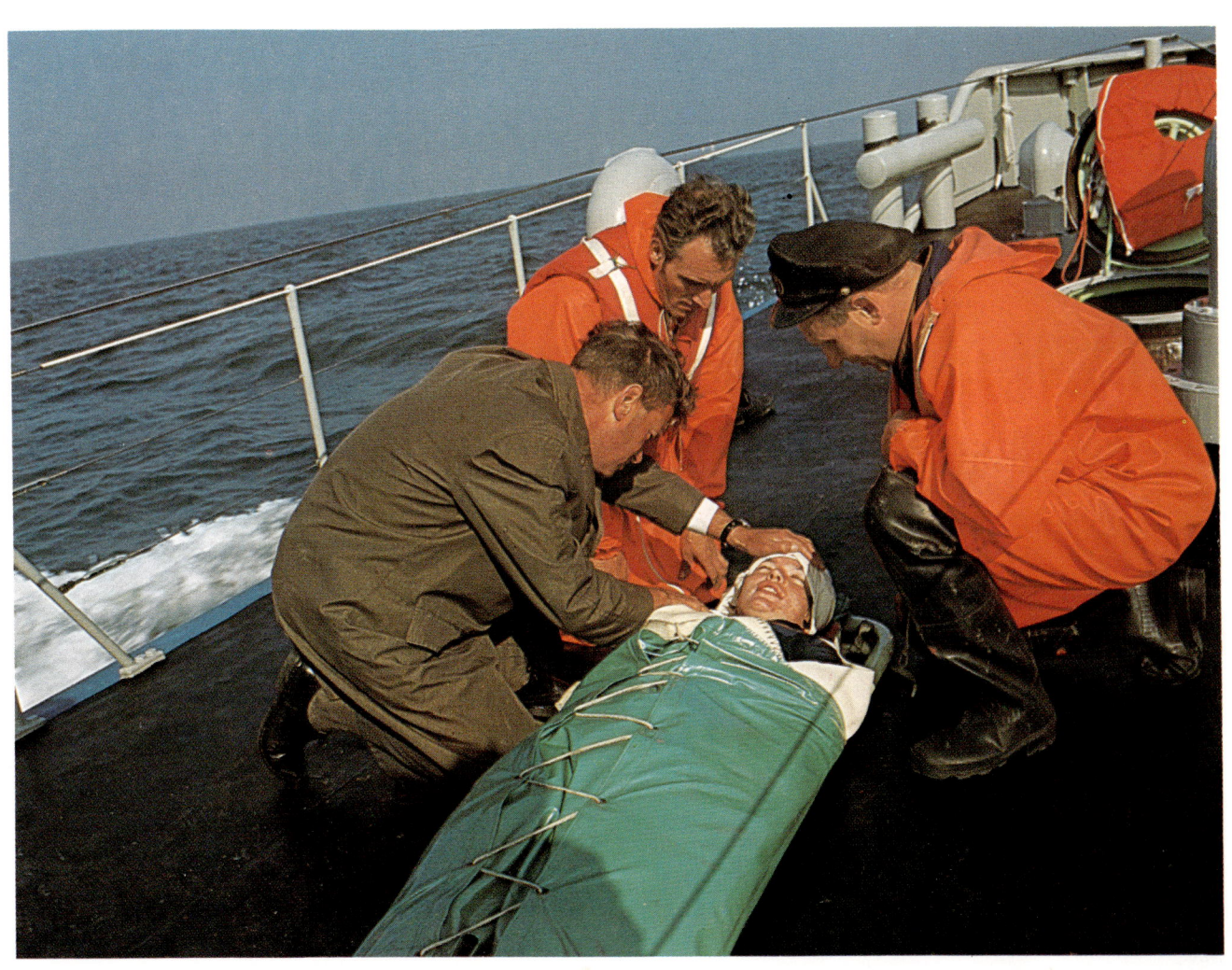

Ports and harbours

Ports and harbours are places where ships can take shelter. Ports are usually large places. Cargo is loaded and unloaded, and passengers go on board. Ships are repaired and made ready for the next voyage. Ports are often built in estuaries where there is plenty of shelter.

Harbours and small ports are used by yachts and pleasure boats, as well as by fishing boats. This harbour is in the Mediterranean.

Large modern ports need deep water so that ocean-going ships can sail in and out. Cargo is stored in warehouses.

This is a small bay in Cornwall in England. It forms a natural harbour. Most of the boats belong to fishermen. They fish near to the shore and bring their catch back home to sell.

Europort is a very modern port built near Rotterdam in Holland. It can take the largest ships.

mussels

RICHES FROM THE SEA

The most important seafood is fish. Millions of tons of fish are caught each year. On this page you can see some of the other sea plants and animals we eat.

The Japanese are very fond of seafood. The people in the picture below are eating a Japanese meal.

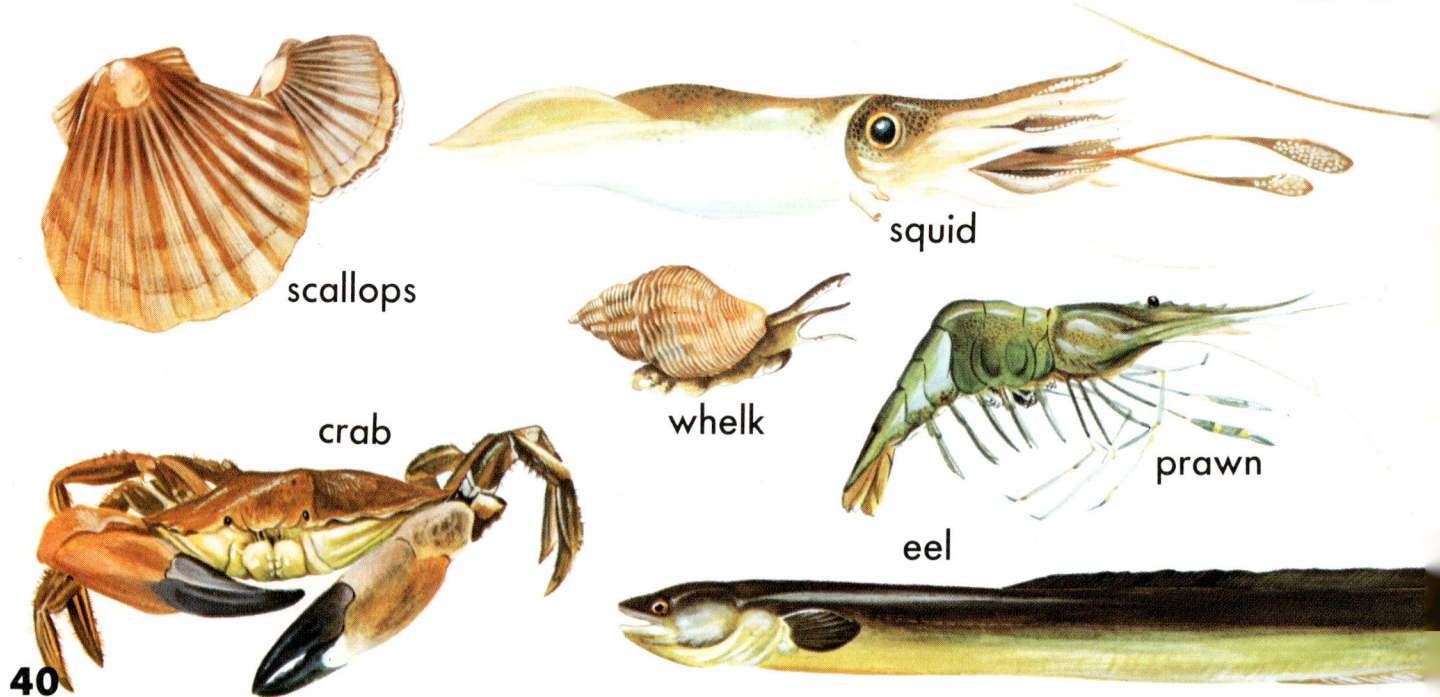

winkles

cockles

scallops

squid

crab

whelk

prawn

eel

Fishermen bring their catch home and lay it out on the beach or quay. Merchants come to see the fish and choose which to buy. They take it to markets or shops to sell.

Fish and other seafoods have to be sold quickly. They are usually sold the same day they are caught.

oyster

seaweed

lobster

shrimp

octopus

Deep-sea fishing

Modern fishing boats catch huge quantities of fish. There are three different ways of deep-sea fishing which you can see in the pictures below.

In some places, divers catch large fish for sport. They use under-water guns to harpoon the fish.

This fishing boat is using a trawl net. The net drags along the sea bed and scoops up the fish.

Drift nets hang like curtains. The fish swim into them and get stuck in the holes.

Modern fishing boats are like floating factories. Winches and cranes are used to pull in and lift the heavy nets full of fish. Once the fish are caught they are frozen on board the ship. The fish have to be frozen immediately. Otherwise they would go bad before the boat gets back to port.

The purse seine is used to enclose a shoal of fish. Then the net is drawn in like a bag.

43

Fish farming

Fishermen have caught so many fish that there are now fewer fish left in the sea. Fish farming is a way of increasing the number of fish for people to eat. The fish are kept in ponds and tanks. They are fed and looked after in the same sort of way that farmers look after cattle and chickens.

Fish eggs and young fish are kept in small tanks. When they are big enough, they are put in large tanks or pools outdoors. Sometimes fish are put in special cages in the sea.

Some kinds of fish farming have been going on for a long time. In the Mediterranean, divers dive to the sea bed and collect living sponges like the ones on the left.

Pearls are formed inside the bodies of oysters. Only a few oysters grow pearls naturally. Oysters grown on farms are all made to form pearls, by putting a grain of sand inside them. When the oysters are fully grown, the pearls are taken out.

45

Treasures from the sea

When ships are wrecked they usually sink. Over the years sand and mud cover the wrecks and help to stop them from rotting away. Divers go down and explore the sea bed. The diver on the right has found some huge old pots, called amphorae.

airbag

suction pipe

The remains of a wreck tell us how ships were built in the past.
The objects on board tell us how people lived in different countries.
This Viking longship is in a museum in Denmark. The Vikings used ships like this for trading.

Everything on an old wreck has to be measured and recorded.
A suction pipe is used to help clear away the mud. All the things that are found are lifted to the surface using airbags and trays.

submersible

tray

PEOPLE AND THE SEA

To stay underwater for a long time people have to wear diving suits. Old fashioned diving suits had large brass helmets and lead boots. Air was pumped down a hose. Today, divers called frogmen wear rubber suits and flippers. They carry air in cylinders which are strapped to their backs.

Modern divers can swim easily underwater. Their suits keep them warm. They can work underwater too. This diver is taking photographs with an underwater camera.

frogman

In Japan, women dive for pearls without special diving equipment. They can go down 30 metres.

Steel suits are needed for the deepest dives. The pressure of the water is very great.

deep-sea diver

50

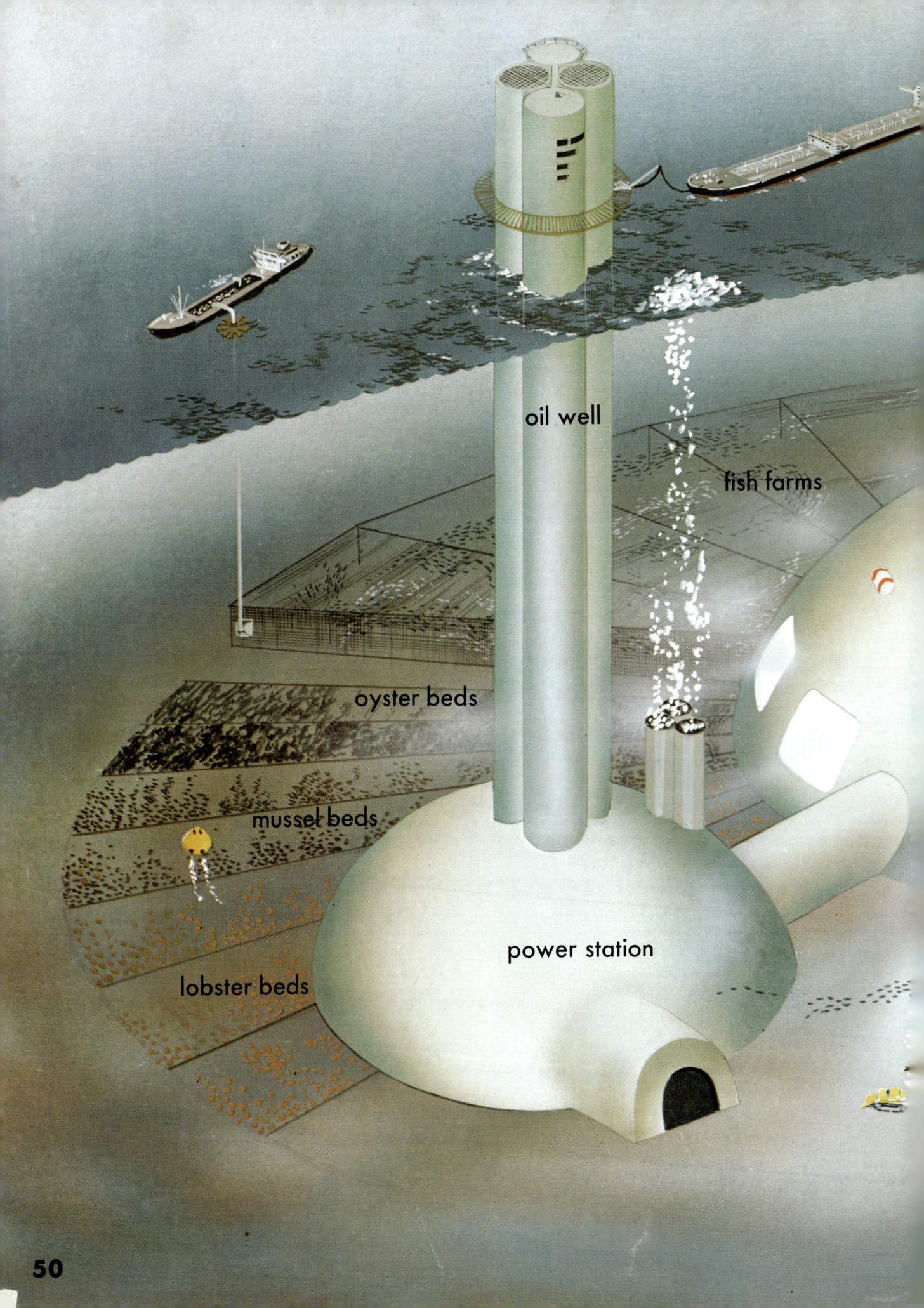

tankers

submarines

underwater town

seaweed farm

Homes under the sea

This is an underwater town of the future, built over an oil well. The oil is pumped to tankers on the surface or into submarines. People living in the underwater town farm fish and grow seaweed on the sea bed. Some people have already lived in buildings underwater for short periods of time.

Save our seas

For a long time people have dumped all kinds of rubbish into the sea. There is so much rubbish that the sea is becoming polluted. Oil spilled by accident from ships and oil rigs kills birds and fish and ruins beaches. Some factories let poisons run into the sea. Sometimes dangerous chemicals are washed overboard from ships. People are now trying to save the oceans from pollution. The sea is the home of many animals, who depend on each other for food. If one dies, others are in danger.

You can help save our sea animals. Next time you go rockpooling learn as much about wildlife as you can, but make sure you leave the pool as you found it. Otherwise, animals will be disturbed. Never take animals home. You should return all creatures to the pool at once.

Many creatures are killed every year by pollution. Others are in danger because they are hunted. People kill whales for their meat, and for their oil, which is used to make perfumes and soaps.

53

Taking land from the sea

Near the coast the sea is often very shallow. In Holland parts of these shallow seas are enclosed by dykes. The sea bed is turned into new land, called polders.

The first step in making new land is to build a dyke. The dyke cuts off an area of shallow seawater.

Most of the water inside the dyke is pumped out. New ground appears. You can see this on the right.

Streams and lakes are left inside the dyke. People cannot walk on the land yet. It is still too soft.

Birds are attracted to the new land. They soon go and nest there.

Soon plants begin to grow, trees are planted and paths are made.

5

The polder is complete. Farmers come to live on the fertile new land. They plant it with many different kinds of crops.

6

Sometimes new land forms by itself. Mud collects behind a sea wall. Slowly the ground rises above sea level, and plants begin to grow. You can see some new land in this picture. At high tide the sea will cover this land.

THE SEA IN HISTORY

Myths and stories about the sea

In the past people knew very little about the sea. Sailors were very superstitious. They made up stories about the strange things they saw. One story was about sea serpents which could attack ships.

There really was a boy who went to school on the back of a dolphin!

sea serpent

Sailors said that they saw mermaids. They thought mermaids were beautiful but very dangerous.

The Ancient Greeks thought there was a god of the sea.

Sirens

The Sirens were creatures from an old Greek legend.

Sailors thought albatrosses brought good luck. It was unlucky to kill these seabirds.

57

Sea battles

There have been many sea battles. Sometimes one country tries to invade another by sea. Sometimes a country attacks another country's trade routes. The first sea battles were fought by soldiers on board ordinary ships. When cannons were invented, ships tried to sink each other at sea.

About four hundred years ago Spain sent a huge fleet of ships to invade England. This fleet was called the Armada. It was destroyed when a big storm blew up. The ships were scattered and the English won the battle. You can see the fight in the big picture.

In this painting you can see an American frigate capturing an English frigate after a long battle.

The German cruiser Scharnhorst destroyed many ships during World War Two. In the end it was sunk.

The navigators

Sailors need to know how to find their way across the sea to other countries. This knowledge is called navigation. While a ship is crossing the sea, sailors often look at their maps and charts. A long time ago, sailors knew their position at sea from looking at the sun and stars. Now they use electronic equipment.

The cross staff helped sailors to work out how far they were from the equator.

The first sailors did not go far away from the land. They could only tell their position by looking at the shape of the coastline.

The Vikings used a portable sundial for navigating. The spike cast a shadow. The sailors set the pointer in the direction they wanted to go.

Later people used sextants. The sextant measures the height of the sun and stars above the horizon. It is very accurate.

Captain Cook used a kind of clock called a chronometer. The clock kept perfect time. It was used to help sailors navigate.

Radar is a great help to modern sailors. It shows a map of the coastline on a screen. Radar also shows the position of other ships, and even large sea animals.

Today, transmitters on shore and satellites above the earth help sailors to navigate. They can show the position, course and speed of a ship very quickly.

Pirates

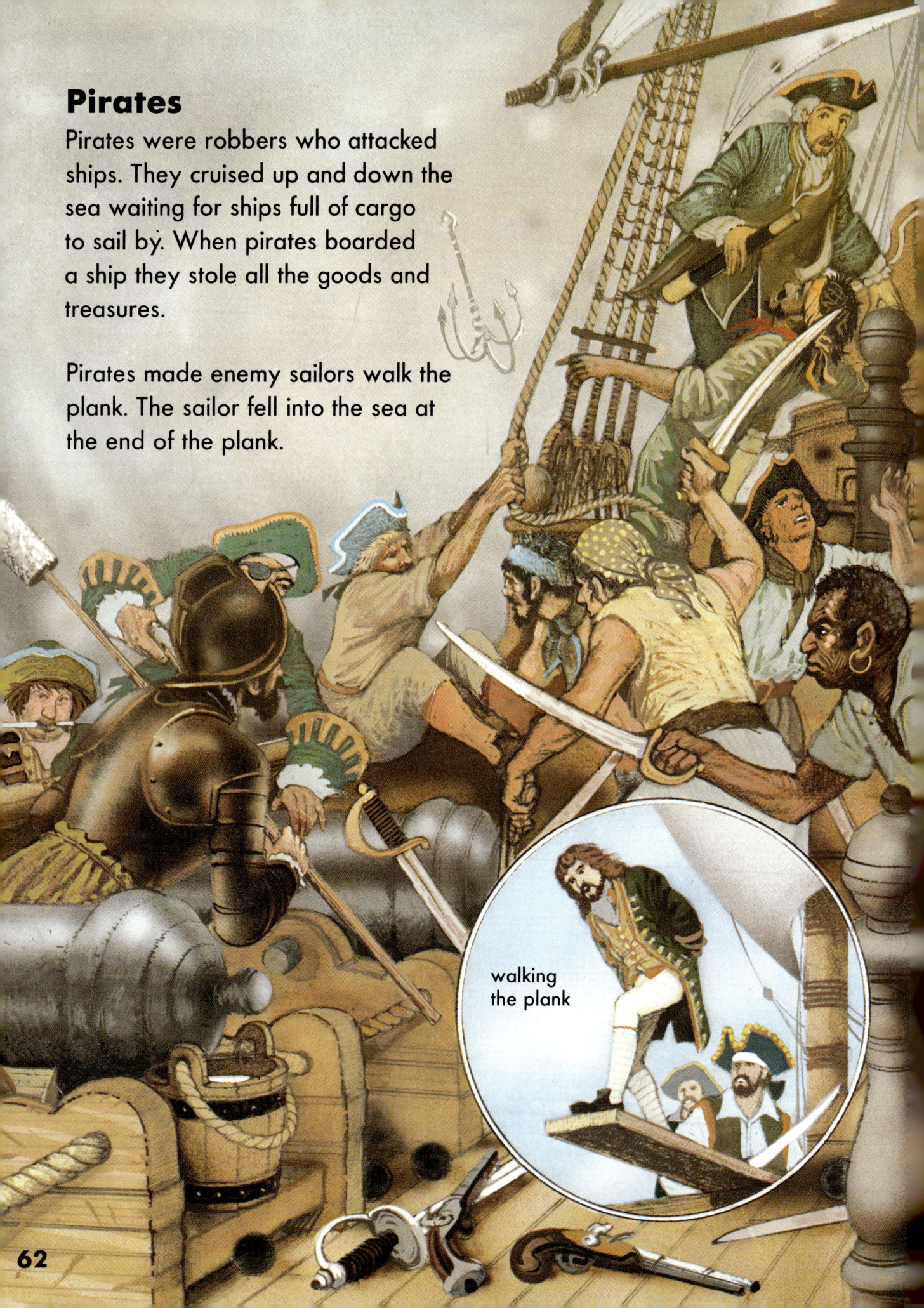

Pirates were robbers who attacked ships. They cruised up and down the sea waiting for ships full of cargo to sail by. When pirates boarded a ship they stole all the goods and treasures.

Pirates made enemy sailors walk the plank. The sailor fell into the sea at the end of the plank.

walking the plank

Pirates buried their treasure in deserted places. A lot of this treasure has never been found.

Many people wanted to put the pirates in prison. The pirates were only safe in places like the Caribbean.

DID YOU KNOW?

One of the most famous pirates was nicknamed Blackbeard. His real name was Edward Teach. He had a dirty black beard and plaited smoking rags in his hair. When he leapt into battle, it looked as though his hair was on fire. His enemies were terrified! He captured many ships before he was caught.

A long time ago, people thought that the earth was flat. No-one dared to sail far away from land. They thought they would fall off the edge of the world! It was a long time before people knew the world was round.

There are some very strange fish living in the deepest parts of the sea. The gulper eel has enormous jaws and a stretchy throat, like elastic. He can swallow animals much bigger than himself. Divers have to be very careful. They have to keep out of the way of dangerous fish.

INDEX

Antarctica   21
Beaufort scale   26-27
Buoys   34
Cliffs   15, 32
Continents   6-7
Coral reefs   18-19
Coves   15, 32
Currents   30-31
Deep-sea fishing   42-43
Dinghy   4, 30
Divers   45, 46, 48-49, 64
Dykes   25, 32, 54-55
Estuaries   16-17
Fish   14-15, 22, 40-45
Fishermen   38, 41, 44
Fish farming   44-45, 51
Fishing nets   42-43
Flooding   24-25
Fresh water   10-11, 16-17
Frogmen   48
Gale   27
Harbours   16, 38-39
Helicopter   37
Hurricane   27
Icebergs   20
Lifeboats   25, 34, 36
Lifejackets   36
Liferaft   36
Lighthouse   4, 34-35
Navigation   60-61

Oceans   6-7, 22-23
Oil   5, 51, 52
Oysters   8, 45
Pearls   45, 49
Pebbly beaches   12-13
Pirates   62-63
Polders   54-55
Pollution   52
Ports   38-39, 43
Radar   61
Rocky shores   14-15
Safety at sea   25, 34-35
Salt water   10-11, 16-17
Sandy beaches   12-13
Sea battles   58-59
Sea bed   5, 9, 42, 45, 46-47, 51
Seabirds   10
Seafood   40-41
Sea rescue   36
Seashore   4, 12, 14
Seaweed   14, 51
Shipwrecks   25, 37, 46-47
Sponges   45
Spring tides   28
Storms   24-25, 27, 58
Submarines   34, 51
Tide   9, 16-17, 28-29, 31
Underwater town   51
Waves   15, 24-25, 26-27, 32
Wind   24, 26-27, 30-31